Anonymous

Flags of Maritime Nations

From the most authentic sources. Fifth Edition

Anonymous

Flags of Maritime Nations
From the most authentic sources. Fifth Edition

ISBN/EAN: 9783337075590

Printed in Europe, USA, Canada, Australia, Japan

Cover: Foto ©ninafisch / pixelio.de

More available books at **www.hansebooks.com**

FLAGS OF MARITIME NATIONS.

FROM THE MOST AUTHENTIC SOURCES.

PREPARED BY ORDER

OF THE

SECRETARY OF THE NAVY

BY THE

BUREAU OF NAVIGATION.

FIFTH EDITION.

WASHINGTON, D. C.
1882.

Resolved by the Senate (the House of Representatives concurring), That there be printed from the plates now in the possession of the Bureau of Navigation, Navy Department, three thousand copies of the "Flags of Maritime Nations," of which eight hundred copies shall be for the use of the Senate; one thousand two hundred copies for the use of the House of Representatives; and one thousand copies for the use of the Navy Department, to be used on board of vessels of the Navy, and for sale at the cost of paper and printing in accordance with section four hundred and thirty-two of the Revised Statutes.

Attest:

F. E. SHOBER, *Acting Secretary.*

In the House of Representatives,

July 28, 1882.

Resolved, That the House concur in the above resolution of the Senate.

Attest:

EWD. McPHERSON, *Clerk.*

LIST OF FLAGS.

PLATE I.

UNITED STATES OF AMERICA.

Ensign.
(A Star for every State.)

President's Flag.
Worn at the main of naval vessels, and in the bow of boats.

A Star for every State

Union Jack.

Flag of the Secretary of the Navy.

Admiral's Flag

Vice Admiral's Flag.

PLATE II.

UNITED STATES — Continued.

Rear Admiral's Flags.   Commodore's Pennants.

Long Pennant.

PLATE III.

UNITED STATES — Continued.

Revenue Flag.

Naval Convoy Flag.

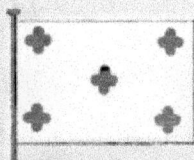

Naval Despatch Flag.

Quarantine Flag.

Heliotype Printing Co. Boston.

PLATE IV.

ARGENTINE REPUBLIC.

Man-of-war Flag and Pennant.

Merchant Flag.

Admiral's Flag

Pilot Flag

PLATE V.

AUSTRIA.

Imperial Standard.

Man-of-war Flag and Pennant.

Grand Admiral's Flag.

Merchant Flag.

Admirals, Vice, and Rear Admiral's Flag.

Commodore's Pennant.

Pilot Flag.

PLATE VI.

BELGIUM.

Royal Standard.

Admiral's and Lieutenant Admiral's Flag.

The Vice Admiral carries the three upper balls.
The Rear Admiral carries the two upper balls.

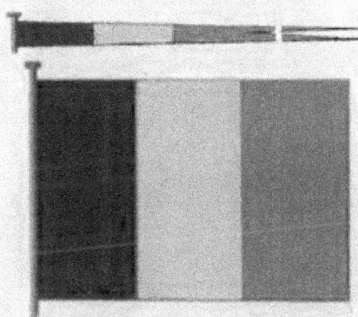

Ensign and Pennant.

Commodore's Pennant.

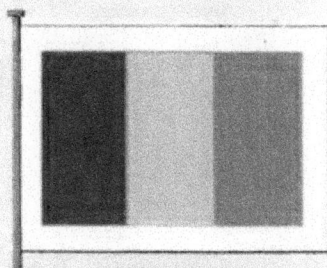

Pilot Flag.

PLATE VII.

BRAZIL.

Imperial Standard.

Admiral's Flag.

Ensign and Pennant.

Commodore's Pennant.

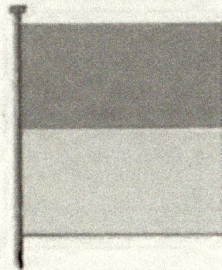

Pilot Flag.

PLATE VIII.

BOLIVIA.

Ensign.

CHILI.

National Standard

Ensign and Pennant

Vice Admirals, Rear Admirals,
and Division Commanders Flag.

CHINA.

Imperial Government Flag.

COREA.

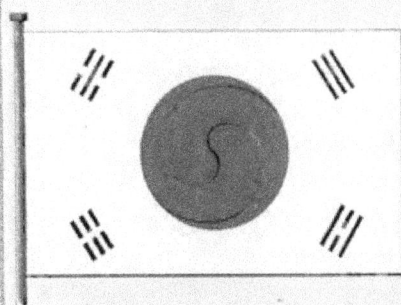

Ensign.

COSTA RICA.

Man-of-war Flag.

Merchant Flag

ECUADOR.

Ensign and Pennant

EGYPT.

Ensign and Pennant.

PLATE X.

DENMARK.

Royal Standard.

Admiral's Flag.

Vice Admiral's Flag.
The Rear Admiral carries two white crosses.

Commodore's Pennant.

Man-of-war Flag and Pennant.

Merchant Flag.

Pilot Flag

PLATE XI.

FRANCE.

Ensign and Pennant.

Admiral's Flag.

Vice Admiral's Flag
In Boats and Tenders

Rear Admiral's Flag.
In Boats and Tenders

Pilot Flag

PLATE XII.

GERMANY.

Imperial Standard.

Man-of-war Flag and Pennant.

Merchant Flag

Pilot Flag.

PLATE XIII.

GREAT BRITAIN.

Royal Standard.

Prince of Wales' Standard

Lord High Admiral's Flag.

Flag of Lord Lieutenant of Ireland.

Flag of Admiral of the Fleet.

Heliotype Printing Co Boston.

PLATE XIV.

GREAT BRITAIN— Continued

Man-of-war Flag and Pennant.

Naval Reserve Flag and Pennant

Merchant Flag.

Admiral's Flag

Vice Admiral's Flag
in Boats and Tenders.
The Rear Admiral carries two red balls.

Commodore's Pennant
1st Class hoisted at the main
2nd Class hoisted at the fore

Pilot Flag

PLATE XV.

GREECE.

Royal Standard.

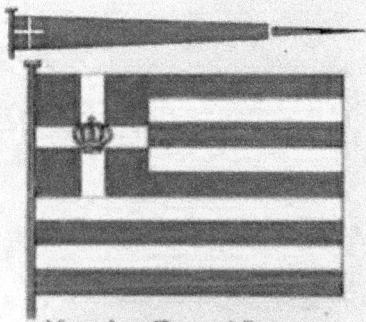

Man-of-war Flag and Pennant.

Merchant Flag.

GUATEMALA.

Man-of-war Flag

Merchant Flag

Heliotype Printing Co. Boston.

PLATE XVI.

HAWAIIAN ISLANDS.

Royal Standard.

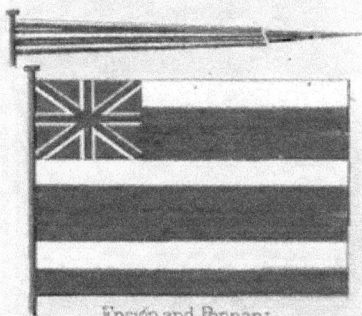

Ensign and Pennant.

HAYTI.

Man-of-war Flag and Pennant.

Merchant Flag.

HONDURAS.

Ensign.

PLATE XVII

ITALY.

Royal Standard.

Man-of-war Flag and Pennant

Admirals Flag.

The Vice Admiral carries the two upper balls
The Rear Admiral carries the upper ball

Commodore's Pennant.

Merchant Flag

Heliotype Printing Co. Boston.

PLATE XVIII.

JAPAN.

Imperial Flag.

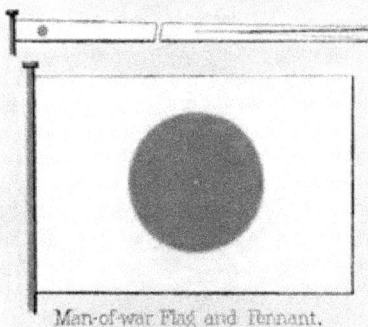

Man-of-war Flag and Pennant.

Admiral's Flag-1st Rank.

Admiral's Flag 2nd Rank.

Admiral's Flag-3rd Rank.

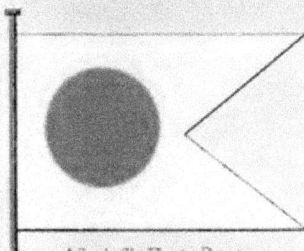

Admiral's Flag-Pro tem.

Pilot Flag.

PLATE XIX.

LIBERIA.

Ensign.

MEXICO.

Man-of-war Flag and Pennant

Admiral's Flag.

Merchant Flag.

Heliotype Printing Co. Boston.

PLATE XX.

MONTENEGRO.

State Flag.

Military Flag.

Marine Flag.

PLATE XXI.

MOROCCO.

Ensign

NETHERLANDS.

Royal Flag

Ensign and Pennant

Admiral's and Lieutenant Admiral's Flag

The Vice Admiral carries three balls
The Rear Admiral carries two balls

Pilot Flag

PLATE XXII.

NORWAY.

Royal Flag.

Man-of-war Flag and Pennant.

Admiral's Flag.

Merchant Flag

Commodore's Pennant.

Pilot Flag.

PLATE XXIII.

NEW ZEALAND.

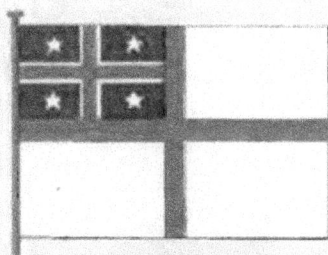

Ensign

NICARAGUA.

Ensign

PARAGUAY.

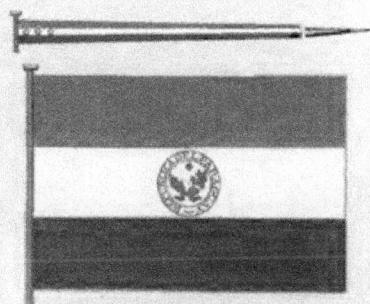

Man-of-war Flag and Pennant

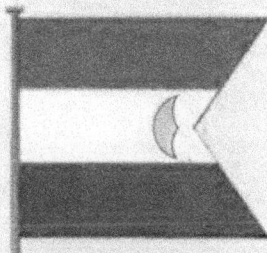

Admiral's Flag

Merchant Flag.

PLATE XXIV

PERSIA.

Ensign.

PERU.

Man-of-war Flag and Pennant.

Merchant Flag.

PLATE XXV.

PORTUGAL.

Royal Flag.

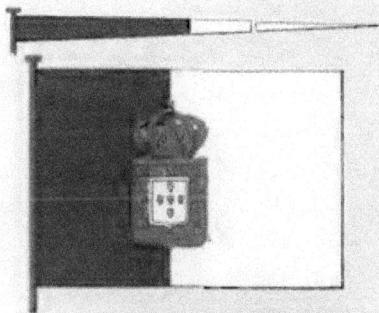

Ensign and Pennant.

Pilot Flag

PLATE XXVI.

RUSSIA.

Imperial Standard.

Man-of-war Flag and Pennant.

Admiral's Flag.
Vice Admiral's Flag has a blue stripe at bottom.
Rear Admiral's Flag a red one

Merchant Flag.

Pilot Flag.

Heliotype Printing Co. Boston.

PLATE XXVII.

SAN DOMINGO.

Man-of-war Flag and Pennant.

Admiral's Flag.

Merchant Flag.

SAN SALVADOR.

Man-of-war Flag.

Merchant Flag.

PLATE XXVIII.

SIAM.

Ensign.

SOCIETY ISLANDS.

Ensign.

SWITZERLAND.

Ensign.

PLATE XXIX.

SPAIN.

Man-of-war Flag and Pennant.

Admiral's Flag.

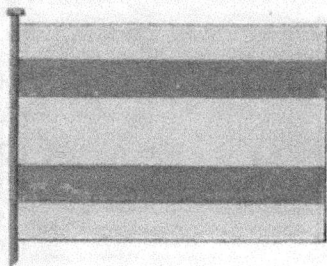

Merchant Flag.

Pilot Flag.

PLATE XXX

SWEDEN.

Royal Flag.

Man-of-war Flag and Pennant.
Admiral's Flag.

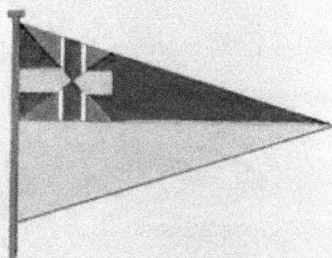

Commodore's Pennant.

Merchant Flag.

Pilot Flag.

PLATE XXXI.

TRIPOLI.

Ensign.

TUNIS.

Man-of-war Flag and Pennant.

Merchant Flag.

TURKEY.

Man-of-war Flag and Pennant.

Merchant Flag.

PLATE XXXII.

UNITED STATES OF COLOMBIA.

Ensign

URUGUAY.

Ensign and Pennant.

VENEZUELA.

Man-of-war Flag and Pennant.

Merchant Flag.